40 DAYS
TO DIVINE WISDOM

THE MIND OF GOD CONTAINED

Apostle Darrell W. Sias

Copyright © 2022 by Darrell Sias

ISBN: 978-1-990695-91-9 (Paperback)

   978-1-990695-92-6 (E-book)

All rights reserved. No part of this publication may be reproduced, distributed, or transmitted in any form or by any means, including photocopying, recording, or other electronic or mechanical methods, without the prior written permission of the publisher, except in the case brief quotations embodied in critical reviews and other noncommercial uses permitted by copyright law.

The views expressed in this book are solely those of the author and do not necessarily reflect the views of the publisher, and the publisher hereby disclaims any responsibility for them. Some names and identifying details in this book have been changed to protect the privacy of individuals.

BookSide Press
877-741-8091
www.booksidepress.com
orders@booksidepress.com

CONTENTS

INTRODUCTION 7
DAY 1: UNSHAKABLE CONFIDENCE 8
DAY 2: POSSESSION.. 9
DAY 3: FAITH: OUR DWELLING PLACE............................ 10
DAY 4: SPIRITUAL DISCERNMENT 11
DAY 5: WORLD-OVERCOMING FAITH.............................. 12
DAY 6: SOWING THE WORD OF GOD 13
DAY 7: SATISFACTION IN CHRIST 14
DAY 8: OVERCOMING POWER 15
DAY 9: FOLLOWING THE EYES OF GOD......................... 16
DAY 10: GOD'S PEACE IS POWER 17
DAY 11: POWER FASTING 19
DAY 12: DIVINE CONNECTIONS.. 20
DAY 13: TAILOR-MADE 21
DAY 14: WISDOM'S AUTHORITY 22
DAY 15: RESPECT FOR AUTHORITIES 23
DAY 16: EYES OF AN EAGLE..24
DAY 17: ENDURING HOPE 25
DAY 18: DOES OF THE WORD 26
DAY 19: PRESERVING POWER 27
DAY 20: DISCERNING OF SPIRITS.....................................28
DAY 21: DIVINE WISDOM 29
DAY 22: JOINTED IN PERFECTION 30
DAY 23: BOLD ADDRESS 31
DAY 24: WISE MASTER BUILDER 32
DAY 25: IT'S A FREE GIFT 33
DAY 26: THE ULTIMATE WARRIOR.................................... 34
DAY 27: MESSENGERS OF CLAY 36
DAY 28: PRESCRIPTION FOR LIVING LIFE 38
DAY 29: YOU ARE NEVER POWERLESS...........................39

DAY 30: UNDIVIDED ATTENTION...................................... 40
DAY 31: NOW SHALL YOUR GOD BE KNOWN............... 41
DAY 32: LIVING IN THE "I AM" 42
DAY 33: ABSOLUTE ALLEGIANCE 43
DAY 34: HIDE AND SEEK... 44
DAY 35: VULNERABLE EMPOWERMENT 46
DAY 36: THE TRUST FACTOR..47
DAY 37: PURIFYING THE SOUL 48
DAY 38: THE REALITY OF VICTORY...................................49
DAY 39: BEHOLDING THE GLORY 50
DAY 40: SUFFERING LAWFULLY 51

APOSTOLIC ORDER THROUGH THE WRITINGS OF PROVERBS..52
    THE INTIMACY OF WISDOM 53
    ACCEPTING INSTRUCTION.. 54
    EQUALITY WISDOM FRUIT BEARING................................. 55
    THE TREASURES OF WISDOM 56
    FOOLISHNESS VERSUS THE WISE IN HEART 57
    JOY IN WISDOM... 58
    COUNSELORS INCREASE LEARNING 59
    POWER IN SONSHIP... 60
    MEN PLAN BUT GOD DIRECTS 61
    CONTENTMENT YIELDS PEACE 62
    WISDOM GIVES ATTENTION TO DETAILS 63
    WISDOM: THE PRINCIPAL THING 64
    THE VOICE OF WISDOM... 65
    THE ORDER OF QUEENS 66
WHY APOSTOLIC PRAYERS?... 68
KEY APOSTOLIC PRAYERS AND PROPHETIC PROMISES

INTRODUCTION

As the Body of Christ, we need to learn what it means to live in *the divine wisdom* of God, this divine wisdom that flows from the divine nature of Christ. What an awesome posture to live in. What an advantage we have over the world's system of life versus the kingdom of God. This devotional is designed to lead you to the place that God originally created in us before sin was. It's time we live in and operate from the divine nature of God. Divine wisdom is what we need in today's chaotic society. Divine wisdom is what we need to move consistently in and with the mind of God. This is the wisdom that created the worlds, the wisdom that spoke and brought shape to all of what God was thinking. This divine wisdom will outlast time and bring us into God's eternal mandate. So strap yourself down and enter into another dimension of living. Forty days from now, you will begin experiencing the order of life that was first intended for us to display in the earth. *Divine wisdom*: take it, possess it; it's your rightful inheritance.

Governing Apostle Darrell W. Sias

DAY 1

UNSHAKABLE CONFIDENCE

This is the confidence that we have in him, that if we ask any thing according to his will, he hears us: And if we know that He hears us, whatsoever we ask, we know that we receive the petitions we desire of him. (1 John 5:14–15)

We are living in the age of the Noah generation. Jesus declared in Matthew 24 that "as the days of Noah were, so shall also the coming of the Son of man be." We must remind ourselves of what is spoken in Genesis 6:5: "And God saw that the wickedness of man was great in the earth, and that every imagination of the thoughts of his heart was only evil continually." Not just man but everything that he created! So here we are in this twenty-first century. Living as it was then, in the now. Evil is looked upon as good and good as evil. We are living in a backward-thinking society. Human life is of little significance. Children are no longer considered precious and valuable. Wickedness is increasing consistently, and it seems as though righteousness is being consumed in the madness.

Where do we, as believers, stand in the midst of all this chaos? What is to be our posture in all this confusion? The Bible says we are to "contend for the faith." Defend the truth as it is in Christ Jesus. Stand up for righteousness, equity, and judgment. This is not possible without total confidence in the lordship of Christ Jesus.

Take your stuff!

Jesus said, "The scripture cannot be broken" (John 10:35).

DAY 2

POSSESSION

Let us hear the conclusion of the whole matter: Fear God and keep his commandments: for this is the whole duty of man. (Ecclesiastes 12:13)

Why possession? Let us hear the sum total of life in God: to respect, honor, and give Him the dignity He deserves. His commandments are his divine order for life. Divine order has to do with that which brings time and eternity together. Divine order connects us with our true ancestry in life. We were born once through Adam, the first man or the first "son of God" in the earth. When Adam sinned, he caused death to pass upon all mankind (Romans 5:12). So instead of mankind being born in the spiritual nature first designed by God, all mankind was born in the fallen nature in Adam. We lost our spiritual connection to God. It is the Word of God through the Holy Spirit of God, spoken into the born again from spirit of man that reunites man to God's original plan and purpose in creation. If we love God, we keep his commandments—his divine order for life.

DAY 3

FAITH: OUR DWELLING PLACE

Now, faith is the substance of things hoped for, the evidence of things not seen. Through faith we understand that the worlds were framed by the word of God, so that things which are seen were not made of things which do appear. (Hebrews 11:1, 3)

*I*n 2 Corinthians 5:7, it says we walk by faith and not by sight.

Faith is a law (**Romans 3:27**). A law is designed to work all the time. So the God kind of faith that we all receive is a spiritual law we are to live by. The Bible says God has dealt to every man the "measure of faith" (**Romans 12:3**). We, as born again believers in Christ Jesus, are given a measure of this spiritual force from God. It is up to us to develop our faith through the **Word of God. In the book of Romans 10:17, it says, "So then faith comes by hearing and hearing by the word of God."** So then faith is a lifestyle for the believer. Faith is of the spirit, and belief is of the mind. The more I feed my spirit man—the spirit life of the Word of God—faith comes. Faith grows and is tested to become strong and active. Now you can see what you say. Our saying always aligns itself with the word of the spirit of life in Christ Jesus.

There's power in your mouth. Speak by faith, not by sight.

DAY 4

SPIRITUAL DISCERNMENT

Beloved, believe not every spirit, but prove the spirits, whether they are of God; because many false prophets are gone out into the world. (1 John 4:1, ASV)

*L*iving in deeper intimacy with the person of truth will cause you to live in deeper discernment with truth. Spiritual discernment is part of the lifestyle of the believer. We don't live our lives out of the natural reasoning of the soul. Our minds are renewed day by day in the spiritual reality of life in Christ. Spiritual discernment is one of the sevenfold anointings or spirits mentioned in the book of **Isaiah 11:2–4**, also in **Revelation 4:5, 5:6.** It is said so often, "God gave us five senses." In the beginning, God gave us of Himself, His spiritual character, his spiritual intelligence. When Adam decided to distrust God and believe Lucifer, he fell from a glorified state to a sinful fallen soul. His mind, will, emotions, intellect, and understanding were given over to a sinful nature. His mind-set was void of spiritual truth. There are many voices in the earth declaring that they are speaking from the mouth of God. How can you know the difference? First, we know the truth in God's Word and have the gift of spiritual discernment. The person of truth, Holy Spirit living in us, gives us the ability to hear clearly the natural from the spiritual. They can speak the exact same words, but those who live by the spirit of discernment know the difference. Our natural senses are not involved. The eyes and ears of the spirit are involved. **Read 1 Corinthians 2:9–11.**

DAY 5

WORLD-OVERCOMING FAITH

For whatsoever is born of God overcomes the world: and this is the victory that overcomes the world, even our faith. (1 John 5:4)

Second Corinthians 4:3–4 states, "But if our gospel be hid, it is hid to them that are lost: In whom the god of this world hath blinded the minds of them which believe not." In Ephesians 2:2, Satan is referred as one who is "the prince of the power of the air, the spirit that now works in the children of disobedience." We understand we need a force, an indwelling power that can overcome all the obstacles and wicked devices of this evil world. It's faith! The born-of-God believer overcomes the world, and the spiritual force by which it is accomplished is faith. We exercise faith in the blood of Jesus, in the power of his resurrection and ascension. The god of this world's system is no match against the faith of the Son of God, Christ Jesus, in us. His faith gives us world-overcoming power.

DAY 6

SOWING THE WORD OF GOD

For he that sows to his flesh shall of the flesh reap corruption; but he that sows to the Spirit shall of the Spirit reap life everlasting. (Galatians 6:8)

You must "sow" the Word of God daily into your soul. Your mind must stay in constant transition to conform into the new life of Christ. Generational strongholds can only be broken through the blood, the word, in the power of Holy Spirit. How do we sow the Word into our heart? Master these pointers and you will begin to see yourself as the powerhouse God has designed:

1. **Verbalization** - speaking the written Word of God and the prophetic Word given by inspiration, creating images (Psalm 45:1).
2. **Visualization** - the crystallization of images through association, making a definite permanent form (Genesis 30:37–31:12).
3. **Internalization** - setting the affections on the Word to cement the vision in the heart or human spirit (Colossians 3:1).
4. **Repetition** - the process of imprinting the vision in the soul (Joshua 1:8).

Follow this process daily and watch your life expand in God's desires for you. Also read Psalms 1:1–6, 5:1, 49:3, 63:5–6, 77:11–12, 119:15, 23, 48.

DAY 7

SATISFACTION IN CHRIST

For in him dwells all the fullness of the Godhead bodily, and you are complete in him, who is "the head of all principality and power. (Colossians 2:9–10)

*The Greek words for "complete" in this passage are the words "**to satisfy**." Let's look at a few definitions that fit in the context of the passage:*

1. To put an end to a desire, want, need, etc., by sufficient or ample provision
2. To give assurance to; convince: to satisfy oneself by investigation
3. To solve or dispel, as a doubt

As believers in Christ, we must mature to the place that our relationship with God has now settled many doubts, confusion, distrust, or unbelief. There should be some absolutes established in our lives. There are to be some undeniable resolves rooted and grounded in us. Our soul is settled and satisfied. We no longer live by the lust of the flesh, lust of the eyes, or the pride of life (**1 John 2:16**). Now Christ is truly grounded in us as the only one who is the head of all principality and power.

Declare your "I Am-ness" in Christ Jesus today. Speak with confident boldness. *I Am* complete, satisfied, and made whole in Christ. Every principality is under my feet.

DAY 8

OVERCOMING POWER

He that overcomes shall inherit all things; and I will be his God, and he shall be my son. (Revelation 21:7)

In Revelation 12:11 it states, "And they overcame him [Lucifer], by the blood of the Lamb and by the word of their testimony." The word *testimony* deals with judicial order. One who displays judicial evidence, deputized to administrate justice in the earth. Allow, enforced, or set by order of a judge. Listen carefully, our testimony isn't so much as telling how God paid my bills and supplied food on my table, etc. All of those are, I suppose, fine in its setting. If any declarations are to be made, any testaments voiced, it should be of the place of empowerment in and through Christ Jesus our Lord. In him we have been deputized to establish spiritual law and order in the heavens and the earth. We have been empowered to administrate righteous judgment and justice in the earth. We have the ordained right to serve injunction against the works of darkness in the earth. We are the "overcomers" in Christ. We are not those who remain repeat offenders. Now we are postured to inherit all things in Christ. Heavenly Father is our God and we are His sons. Hallelujah.

DAY 9

FOLLOWING THE EYES OF GOD

I will instruct thee and teach thee in the way which thou shalt go: I will counsel thee with mine eye upon thee. (Psalm 32:8)

Throughout the New Testament, especially in the book of Revelation, Jesus makes the statement, "He that has an ear to hear let him hear." Now the second *hear* is defined in the Greek as "to understand." Proverbs 4:5 explains that we must pursue wisdom; it's a necessary component, but in all our acquiring, we need to get an understanding also. The word *understanding* in the Greek is **defined as "discernment, to become intelligent."** In order to be taught the paths of God for our direction in life, in order to receive and understand his counsel, we need to "discern," have spiritual intelligence in what he says to us. God is counseling us with His eye. His perception, understanding, and definition of life is different from ours. God is infinite; he's eternal. We are born again of his Spirit but are living in time. So we must, as spirit people, understand, discern, and have spiritual intelligence of how he sees life on earth for us. Praying in the spirit, the Bible says, will build us up in our most holy faith. We are empowered in our spirit, but also we tap into divine wisdom with our Father's perception of the eternal inheritance he has given us through his Son. Read also 1 Corinthians 2:9–16.

DAY 10

GOD'S PEACE IS POWER

Peace I leave with you; my peace I give unto you: not as the world gives, give I unto you. Let not your heart be troubled, neither let it be fearful. (John 14:27)

In Mark 4, Jesus began teaching a parable about a sower who went out into a field to sow. As illustrated, the sower sowed on four different types of soil or ground. Jesus had to later explain to his disciples what the moral of the story was. He made a striking statement that will lead us to understand how we are to possess His kind of peace. In verse 13 Jesus says, "Know you not this parable? How then will you know all parables?" What? You mean, if I don't understand the parable of the sower, I will not understand any other teachings that Jesus taught while on earth? You mean, I will not understand the doctrine of Christ? His next words were the sower sows the *word*. Then he goes on to describe the types of ground, illustrating the souls of man. Later in the chapter beginning in verse 35, Jesus gets in a boat with his disciples and tells them, "Let's go to the other side." A storm arose while he was in the back of the boat asleep. In much fear, they woke him up screaming at him that he doesn't care that they are about to perish. You know the story.

Jesus gets up and rebukes the elements, and everything settled into calm. Then he rebukes them because they had no faith, no Word sown in their hearts. The Creator of the wind, water, and rain was in the boat asleep. The storm disturbed their peace, but their fear and faithlessness disturbed His peace. Ask the Holy Spirit to examine the "ground" of your heart.

Has the Word been sown on good ground to bring about a bountiful harvest where God's peace is reigning powerfully in you? Or is it still so cluttered that the Word sown cannot grow? Read Mark 4:1–41.

DAY 11

POWER FASTING

Is this not the fast I choose: to release the bonds of injustice, to untie the ropes of the yoke, and to let the oppressed go free, and tear every yoke to pieces? Is it not to break your bread for the hungry? You must bring home the poor, the homeless. When you see the naked, you must cover him, and you must not hide yourself from your relatives. Then your light shall break forth like the dawn, and your healing shall grow quickly. And your salvation shall go before you; the glory of Yahweh will be your rear guard. (Isaiah 58:6–8)

This is the fast of all fast. A fast that can pull you away from what may have become just a ritual, a fast that no longer produces change in you. Has your fast become stale before God? Is your soul in the same condition as it was before the fast and this is your tenth time around? Let's break tradition somewhat and ask the Holy Spirit to put you on a fast that He will choose. You will lose the bonds of wickedness, undo heavy burdens; let the oppressed go free and that you break every yoke. Now selfishness, faultfinding, anger, pride, and the works of the flesh are out of your way. You now are free to minister to the bound, confused, insane, hungry, naked, and homeless. Wait, you can't forget your own flesh anymore, the family members you have ignored for so long a time. Read and absorb verses 7–12. Reap your harvest.

DAY 12

DIVINE CONNECTIONS

For if while we were enemies we were reconciled to God through the death of His Son, much more, having been reconciled, we shall be saved by His life. (Romans 5:10)

We have been delivered, rescued, and freed from bondage. The divine order in releasing the *eternal word* to become flesh to reconcile all mankind back to him is astounding. It would take a supernatural encounter to accomplish this task. God choosing to disregard the outlandish hatred and disrespect against his magnificent love by reconciling us through the death of Jesus is mind-boggling. One would have to grow in relationship with him and his Word in beginning to fully understand the depths of the wickedness of sin. As a whole, we take the sacrifice that God made in sending his only begotten Son to mankind to allow him to be so mocked and beat up that the scripture says, "His visage was marred that he was unrecognizable." Then kill him because death was the ransom required to redeem mankind back to him. So now you must see the depth and power of your reconciled life in Christ. You must understand and grab hold of how valuable you are to God for him to go to lengths to save you when you didn't have a clue of the depths of your bondage. So the next time you doubt that he loves you, cares for you, and hears you when you pray, just remember this: "For God so loved the world [you] that he gave his ONLY begotten Son that whosoever believes in him should not perish but have everlasting life."

DAY 13

TAILOR-MADE

I will greatly rejoice in the LORD, my soul shall be joyful in my God; for he hath clothed me with the garments of salvation, he hath covered me with the robe of righteousness, as a bridegroom decked himself with ornaments, and as a bride adorned herself with her jewels. (Isaiah 61:10)

One must spend time in deep thought with the Word of God. When you read passages such as this, you cannot just run through it casually. For instance, "My soul shall be joyful." He didn't say his spirit shall be joyful, but his soul shall be joyful. That means that he had to bring his mind to a place to be joyful in God in spite of what was happening around him. Regardless of the circumstance, his soul would not be given over to his emotions. How could this be? Listen, here's the answer. He *knew* that God had clothed him with His salvation as with a garment, and His righteousness was around him like a robe. It doesn't stop there, as a bridegroom decks himself with ornaments, and a bride adorns herself with her jewels. I challenge you to take this to the secret chamber of meditation and intimacy with God, the Holy Spirit. Write of your own experience. **Read Psalm 145.**

DAY 14

WISDOM'S AUTHORITY

The fear of the Lord is the beginning of knowledge. Stubborn fools despise wisdom and discipline. (Proverbs 1:7)

Fearing the Lord God is the beginning of knowledge. To fear God is to give him high honor and ultimate respect and reverence. This is a deep state of mind. Your inner thoughts are so shaped in this reality that your body feels the posture and position of your mind. It's in this posture that acquiring knowledge in God begins. Understanding the authority he exhibits in the heavens and the earth qualifies you to respect him highly. It will qualify you as a candidate for impartation. It brings discipline in your life, dedication, and diligence. You gain authority over your mind, your thought life. A part of the verse says, "Stubborn fools despise wisdom and discipline." A stubborn person is unteachable, hard to reach, undisciplined. The fear of God puts you in a place of authority and power in exercising his wisdom. You won't ignore, despise, or make fun of those who live well-ordered, disciplined lives. True power is displayed when one has authority over his thought life. Step into another dimension in the mind of God. Read Proverbs 4. Emphasis is on verse 23.

DAY 15

RESPECT FOR AUTHORITIES

Let every soul be subject unto the higher powers. For there is no power but of God: the powers that be are ordained of God. Whosoever therefore resists the power resist the ordinance of God: and they that resist shall receive to themselves damnation. (Romans 13:1–2)

The ordinance of God is the accurate arrangement of things, a disposition. A disposition in this context would be the predominant or prevailing tendency of one's spirit or mind. Where is the state of your mind regarding the power of God? Let every *soul* be subject unto. Let every soul be submitted to God's power. *Submitted* means to give over or yield to the power or authority of another, to defer to another's judgment, opinion, or decision. *All* the powers that be are ordained of God. The word *power* here is the Greek word "exousia" or authority, one who exercises authority in judicial affairs. The apostle Paul is mainly focusing on the natural judicial order set in the earth to keep the peace. Our police force for instance. How can we obey God in all things if we don't obey the laws of the land and don't respect those who have been given charge over our natural environment? We are guilty of speeding, running red lights, etc. If we can't obey the earthly, how can we obey the spiritual? By being lawless in our responsibilities in the earth, what does it reveal about how we keep God's order in spiritual matters? Read Romans 13:1–14.

DAY 16

EYES OF AN EAGLE

But the end of all things is at hand: be ye therefore sober, and watch unto prayer. (1 Peter 4:7)

In Luke 18:1, Jesus began to teach a parable in relation to prayer. He said, "Men ought always to pray and not to faint." The essence of his words were to address having a specific mind-set in regards to answered prayer. The widow in the story was so persistent in the story that her consistent persistence caused a hard-hearted judge to grant her the desired partition; verse 5 says, "Because this widow troubles me, I will avenge her, lest by her continual coming she weary me." The word *faint* in this context means "**to be utterly spiritless, to be wearied out, exhausted.**" We the believers in Christ have entered into a time of much agitation and conflict in the spirit realm. It is God's desire that we are in tune to His mind and power at all times. "The end of all things is at hand," this statement is absolutely in the now. We are not looking for this age to come; we are *here*! So let's take three key words Jesus spoke in Luke 18 and apply it to the apostle Peter's remarks. It's the word **avenge.** To avenge means "to vindicate one's right, to protect, defend, do one justice." Couple this with being sober (to be of sound mind, to exercise self-control). Watch unto prayer. Be circumspect, discreet, and prudent. In other words, don't let outside situations and circumstances divert you from having intense, focused faith, an established agenda, and purposeful intent when coming before the heavenly courts in prayer. Never allow the conditions of this present world negate the power of the eternal world of the Spirit: the kingdom of God.

DAY 17

ENDURING HOPE

> Now the God of hope fill you with all joy and peace in believing, that ye may abound in hope, through the power of the Holy Ghost. (Romans 15:13)

The joy of the Lord is our strength (Nehemiah 8:10a). John 14:27 states, "Peace I leave with you, my peace I give unto you ... let not your heart be trouble neither let it be afraid." Romans 5:20b–21 states, "Where sin abound grace did much more abound; that as sin hath reign unto death, even so might grace reign through righteousness unto eternal life by Jesus Christ our Lord." Acts 1:8 states, "And you shall receive power after that the Holy Ghost is come upon you." We are never without the eternal Word of God. The apostle Paul wrote in Colossians 1:9 "that we might be filled with the knowledge of his will in all wisdom and spiritual understanding [being fruitful in every good work, and increasing in the knowledge of God]." Last but not least, the writer in Hebrews 1:3, in pertaining to the power of the Word of Christ over us, states, "Upholding all things by the word of his power, when he had by himself purged our sins, sat down on the right hand of the majesty on high." We have *enduring hope* in Christ that cannot be shaken or removed; it is from everlasting to everlasting. Read Ephesians 1.

DAY 18

DOERS OF THE WORD

Therefore whosoever hears these sayings of mine, and does them, I will liken him unto a wise man, which built his house upon a rock: And the rain descended, and the floods came, and the winds blew, and beat upon that house; and it fell not: for it was founded upon a rock. (Matthew 7:24–25)

In this discourse as Jesus was speaking, known as the Sermon on the Mount, he says in verse 21 of Matthew 7, **"Not everyone that says unto me, Lord, Lord, shall enter into the kingdom of heaven; but he that does the will of my Father which is in heaven."** We, the Body of Christ, sometimes pride ourselves on our ability to quote multiple verses of scripture. That may sound good on the surface, but it seems we are guilty of more scripture memorization than word *internalization*. We sound very spiritual, but our lifestyles prove differently. We say a lot, but manifest little. Jesus is placing emphasis on the hearers and doers. Those who *do* what he says will be established upon a rock. Jesus is that rock. Those who are of the world need to see the power of a stable-minded believer, "You will keep him in perfect peace whose mind is stayed on me: because he trusts in me" (Isaiah 26:3). Also read James 1:22–25.

DAY 19

PRESERVING POWER

And we know that the Son of God is come, and hath given us an understanding, that we may know him that is true, and we are in him that is true, even in his Son Jesus Christ. This is the true God, and eternal life. Little children, keep yourselves from idols. Amen. (1 John 5:20–21)

Jude declared in verse 24 and 25 of the book, "Now unto him that is able to keep you from falling, and to present you faultless before the presence of his glory with exceeding joy, to the only wise God our Savior, be glory and majesty, dominion and power, both now and forever. Amen."

John the Beloved, as he is known, also wrote in verse 4 and 5 of chapter 5, "For whatsoever is born of God overcomes the world: and this is the victory that overcomes the world, even our faith. He that believes that Jesus is the Son of God?" By God's grace (his divine influence upon the heart and its reflection in the life), we have been saved. We must have a revelation of Jesus Christ and what in him being "man" has done for us and being in being God has established in us.

Read Ephesians 1 and 2.

DAY 20

DISCERNING OF SPIRITS

Beloved, believe not every spirit, but try the spirits, whether they are of God; because many false prophets are gone out into the world. (1 John 4:1)

Try the spirits to test, examine, prove, and scrutinize (to see whether a thing is genuine or not). Our atmosphere, the world in which we live, is filled with all manner of speech—words that are trying to find its way into our souls, whether good or evil. "OK," you might say, "I know the Word of God. I know the difference between right and wrong." Wonderfully put. So for a moment, put your great assurance aside and take note of what the prophetic apostle is saying. Believe not every *spirit*. Let's put some definition to this word in particular. The Greek word "pneuma" here refers to the rational soul, the way in which a human being feels, thinks, and decides. It also points to the mind of God, His character, his personality. So if we are hearing and listening to words spoken from someone who says they are sent from God or voices in the atmosphere trying to gain access into our thought life, we need to be able to *know* who is speaking. We need this *gift* of God given to us by the Holy Spirit to operate as citizens of His kingdom. This is a spiritual gift, empowering you to live beyond your natural mind, your five senses. You *must* exercise this powerful gift. Your natural mind cannot comprehend spiritual things. Read Romans 8.

DAY 21

DIVINE WISDOM

So teach us to number our days, that we may apply our hearts unto wisdom. (Psalm 90:12)

Number has to do with "setting things in order." We need structure and alignment. Teach us to "set" our days in order, that we can apply our "minds" to God's wisdom (Proverbs 16:1–3).

The Word of God is filled with scriptures that speak concerning the believer obtaining wisdom. It is "the principal thing" (Proverbs 4:7). Here is the writer who is pointing wisdom in a certain direction. We need wisdom in learning to live strategically, structurally. We should be a people who plan our hours, days, weeks, and months carefully. We don't just exist in this world; God has a specific plan for our lives. We must on purpose become inundated with wisdom to correctly bring order to the place where chaos wants to exist. We must demand an atmosphere of discipline and order. If we live without direction, how will we ever know the will of God for our lives? How will we ever know if we are following the course he has directed for us? Stop living by instinct. Stop following a routine that leads to nowhere each and every day. Step out of the world; wind a pointless lifestyle into a purposeful lifestyle. Live a life that causes you to be like your heavenly Father—creative, resourceful, and productive. Live on course.

DAY 22

JOINTED IN PERFECTION

Now I beseech you, brethren, by the name of our Lord Jesus Christ, that ye all speak the same thing, and that there be no divisions among you; but that ye be perfectly joined together in the same mind and in the same judgment. (1 Corinthians 1:10)

We are the Body of Christ. We are one body and one blood in Christ Jesus. The Word says in Hebrews 10:5, "A body hast thou prepared me." It further explains in the preceding verses that it wasn't the bodies of bulls and goats that should take away sins. It was Christ's physical body that was offered up for us. He won our victory by conquering in His physical body. His body became sin for us that we might become his righteousness. We must begin to see ourselves as *one* body in Christ Jesus. This way, the world who should be on the outside looking inside should hear one voice in Christ. We must align ourselves with the truth of the Word and our personal preferences. The Word of God is our final authority. Read 1 Corinthians 12.

DAY 23

BOLD ADDRESS

The LORD is nigh unto all them that call upon him, to all that call upon him in truth. He will fulfil the desire of them that fear him: he also will hear their cry, and will save them. (Psalm 145:18–19)

Release all your heart to the Father. It doesn't matter what He already knows. It's what we have—the confidence in knowing and expecting Him to respond because of His *great love* for us. His *great love* for you. Express your whole heart unto Him. He's waiting for you.

1 John 5:14–15, "And this is the confidence that we have in him, that, if we ask any thing according to his will he hears us: and if we know that he hears us, whatsoever we ask, we know that we have the petitions that we desired of him."

DAY 24

WISE MASTER BUILDER

For every house is built by some man; but he that built all things is God. (Hebrews 3:4)

Your "inner" being is the "house" God wants and needs to be the builder of. Are you allowing him to build your mind to see things as he sees them, understand things as He understands them, define and interpret life as He does? Study to show yourself approved unto God. Prayer without the Word of God is unfruitful. The Word of God without *prayer* is unfruitful. They go hand in hand. You'll be amazed at what will happen when you allow the wise master builder to reconstruct the house he originally made before sin was. Now build your world on the Word of God alone. It's your only sure foundation. Second Timothy 2:19 states, "The foundation of the God stands sure having this seal; The Lord knows them that are his. And, let everyone that names the name of Christ depart from iniquity."

DAY 25

IT'S A FREE GIFT

For the grace of God has been revealed, bringing salvation to all people. (Titus 2:11)

*S*alvation—to rescue, to deliver, to prosper, to make whole, etc.

Ask yourself this question: Have I truly received the *free* gift God has given me through His Son? I'm being delivered from the things that hunt me and seem to follow me from week to week, month to month, year to year! If so, it's time to put it to an end. By *grace*, you have been saved; it is a gift. Just accept and conform to the gift of God's grace. It's the power of God in Christ Jesus to us and in us and for us. Stop struggling with the works of religion. Accept, receive, and live it by faith. Read Romans 5.

DAY 26

THE ULTIMATE WARRIOR

The LORD is a man of war: the LORD is his name. (Exodus 15:3)

The Lord is always our present help in time of need, the scriptures say, our very present help. We must know our God has established our victory in Christ Jesus once and for all. The prophet spoke to Jehoshaphat and all the people that they would not have to fight in that particular battle, but stand still and see the salvation of the Lord for you (emphasized). Let us first examine the word *war*. **War in Hebrew means "in the sense of fighting; the engagement, warfare, a battle, warrior fighting." It comes from a root word meaning "to feed on, consume, devour, eat, fight, overcome, and prevail."**

This was a song of Moses and the children of Israel after they had crossed the Red Sea and witnessed the hand of God perform a supernatural feat that cannot be called any other way. Their former oppressors and enslavers as well as Pharaoh's elite soldiers were consumed in the Red Sea. Never to be seen again. In fact, Moses told the people, "For the Egyptians whom you have seen today, you shall see them again no more forever." They were consumed, devoured, and destroyed. God prevailed, overcame, and devoured His enemies. We as the Body of Christ, the born again from above family of God who do *know* our God, must come to the place of knowing who it is we pray to. We know that God cannot lie but remains true to Himself. Your enemies already have their destination settled by God. It's a done deal. God loves to pick a fight and put us in the midst to exercise His great dominion and power in the earth in our behalf. So stop fretting over trouble, attacks, hardships, and the stuff we call warfare; that's many times no more than an oppressed state of the soul. If there's ever the spirit of death knocking at life's door in the many forms that death operates out of, you can rest assure that Jesus has already fought and conquered death in your behalf.

DAY 27

MESSENGERS OF CLAY

How beautiful on the mountains are the feet of the messenger who brings good news, the good news of peace and salvation, the news that the God of Israel reigns! (Isaiah 52:7)

ut we have this treasure in earthen vessels that the excellency of the power may be of God and not of ourselves. (1 Corinthians 4:7)

To open their eyes, and to turn them from darkness to light, and from the power of Satan unto God, that they may receive forgiveness of sins, and inheritance among them which are sanctified by faith that is in me. (Acts 26:18)

I charge you therefore before God, and the Lord Jesus Christ, who shall judge the quick and the dead at his appearing and his kingdom; Preach the word; be instant in season, out of season; reprove, rebuke, exhort with all longsuffering and doctrine. (2 Timothy 4:1–2)

Go you therefore, and teach all nations, baptizing them in the name of the Father, and of the Son, and of the Holy Ghost: Teaching them to observe all things whatsoever I have commanded you: and, lo, I am with you always, even unto the end of the world. Amen. (Matthew 28:19–20)

And when they had preached the gospel to that city, and had taught many, they returned again to Lystra, and to Iconium, and Antioch, confirming the souls of the disciples, and exhorting them to continue in the faith, and that we must through much tribulation enter into the kingdom of God. (Acts 14:21–22)

Then Peter said unto them, repent and be baptized every one of you in the name of Jesus Christ for the remission of sins, and you shall receive the gift of the Holy Ghost. For the promise is unto you, and to your children, and to all that are afar off, even as many as the Lord our God shall call, and with many other words did he testify and exhort, saying, save yourselves from this untoward generation. (Acts 2:38–40)

DAY 28

PRESCRIPTION FOR LIVING LIFE

Finally, brethren, whatsoever things are true, whatsoever things are honest, whatsoever things are just, whatsoever things are pure, whatsoever things are lovely, whatsoever things are of good report; if there be any virtue, and if there be any praise, think on these things. (Philippians 4:8)

Religion has added so many do's and don'ts to living life in Christ Jesus that it's no wonder people do not want to become a part of the Body of Christ. Man with his finite mind has tried to define the *most powerful eternal entity* to ever exist. Notice I did not say *one* of the most powerful. I said *the* most powerful. We are a celestial order brought to the earth by and in Christ Jesus, God become flesh, Emmanuel, God with us. We have been born again from above of incorruptible seed. Do we stop and just study the Word of God for ourselves. The prophet Micah summed it up this way, "What does the Lord require of you, but to do justly, and to love mercy, and to walk humbly with your God?" **(Micah 6:8).** What we read in Philippians is a clear picture of God's character. His nature placed in us through Christ by the Holy Spirit. We are a "new creation" of God in the earth as it is in heaven. We have been saved by *grace* through faith. Grace is the divine influence on the heart (mind) and its reflection in the life. So as we are growing into maturity with God and His Word, he is making known to you who He is in you through grace. He says, "Let's keep it simple or easy to understand; if it's true, honest, justifiable, pure, lovely, can carry a good report of moral excellence, and is praiseworthy, *think* on these things. Meditate deeply."

DAY 29

YOU ARE NEVER POWERLESS

Have you never heard? Have you never understood? The Lord is the everlasting God, the Creator of all the earth. He never grows weak or weary. No one can measure the depths of his understanding. He gives power to the weak and strength to the powerless. (Isaiah 40:28–29)

You are never without power, spiritually, physically, mentally, or emotionally. You have power on demand. The Bible says in Ephesians 2:6, speaking of the believer in Christ, "And has raised us up together and made us sit together in heavenly places in Christ Jesus." The Greek word definition for *sit* means "to give (or take) a seat in company with; (make) sit (down) together." It comes from a root word denoting "union with or together by association; completeness." In chapter 1 of Ephesians verses 19–23, the apostle Paul gives us to understand that God the Father, when raising Christ from the dead, set him far above all principality and power, and that we are his body, the fullness of him that fills all in all. "Have you never read? Are you still without understanding?" Read Ephesians chapters 1 and 2.

DAY 30

UNDIVIDED ATTENTION

Then Jesus said, "Come to me, all of you who are weary and carry heavy burdens, and I will give you rest." (Matthew 11:28)

This scripture in context deals with the weights of religious sanctions through the law of Moses, but the principle can be used to break physical, mental, and emotional burdens as well. We as the Body of Christ should learn to live in the finished work of Christ. Meaning, what His death, burial, resurrection, and ascension accomplished for us. What liberty, peace, soundness of mind, power, and strength are you to live in. The entire Word speaks of Christ Jesus, yes, so what are we doing with the Word of God past scripture memorization? For the majority of the Body of Christ, we come short with sound, solid, intense, meditation on the Word of God. So our minds are not really transformed into the living bread of life. Without transformation into spirit reality in the spirit of Christ, we cannot comprehend what real power is in Christ. We cannot possess the true place of peace in God through a carnal or natural way of thinking. "Because the carnal mind is enmity [hatred and hostility] against God, it is not subject to the law [divine order] of God, neither indeed can be. So then they that are in the flesh [carnal reasoning] cannot please God" (Romans 8:7–8).

It's time to be true to ourselves and question why and what is keeping you from living the abundant life that Jesus died for and was raised from the dead to give unto you. The Holy Spirit is waiting for your presence to get quiet with Him that he may give you the keys to unlock the door that's keeping you out of the peace of God. Are you truly born again from above? Read John 3 and Romans 8.

DAY 31

NOW SHALL YOUR GOD BE KNOWN

How great you are, O Sovereign Lord! There is no one like you. We have never even heard of another God like you! (2 Samuel 7:22)

This generation of Noah will challenge you to know the god you say you pray to. This is an age where there's a famine for the Word of God. This famine for the truth of God's Word to be revealed will be fed out of the abundance of God's goodness concerning His new creation. The god of the Bible has scarcely preached and demonstrated long enough. The person of truth Christ Jesus has been suppressed long enough. It's time you hear the sound of the abundance of God's grace and force in the wind of His presence. This is the age to live in the words of the apostle Peter, "Repent therefore and be converted, that your sins may be blotted out, when the times of refreshing shall come from the presence of the Lord" (Acts 3:19). Be now endued with power from on high. Be filled with the abundant power and authority of Christ Jesus, the Apostle and High Priest of your profession. Let His sovereign order possess your will as you release full ownership of your life to him. Refuse to live without the foundation of the kingdom in you. Righteousness, peace, and joy in Holy Ghost.

DAY 32

LIVING IN THE "I AM"

The LORD is my rock, and my fortress, and my deliverer; my God, my strength, in whom I will trust; my buckler, and the horn of my salvation, and my high tower. (Psalm 18:2)

We are Christ's, and Christ is God's. "Herein is *your* [emphasis added] love make perfect, that *you* [emphasis added] may have boldness in the Day of Judgment because as He [Christ] is, so are you in this world" as paraphrased in 1 John 4:17. Your life is hid with Christ in God. Christ is the "I Am," all that you need or can desire. He is your complete satisfaction. Colossians 2:10 declares, "And you are complete in Him who it the head of all principality and power." This Greek word *complete* means to be satisfied. The word *power* speaks of having territorial rule by a prince. You must now receive His complete provision for you and how you are to operate in the authority of all that He is. You must begin to speak with bold confidence and say, "Jesus, you are that, I am also." God sees you through the victory his son Jesus conquered for you. He conquered sin in His flesh for you. He completed what you could never do. Every time you pray, every time you want to have a fellowship with God the Holy Spirit, you have clear access because of Jesus and His finished work. He's the "horn" of your salvation. **Receive it by speaking it until you have it within you, then you will see it before you.**

DAY 33

ABSOLUTE ALLEGIANCE

For I am sure that neither death nor life, nor angels nor rulers, nor things present nor things to come, nor powers, nor height nor depth, nor anything else in all creation, will be able to separate us from the love of God in Christ Jesus our Lord. (Romans 8:38–39)

re you able to confess this with your *whole* heart now? Can you stand in this posture with and in the unrestrained power of Christ by Holy Spirit in you? Do you have bold confidence in Him to this measure? If not now, arise and challenge yourself to step into this place of honor in and with Christ. Your commitment to prayer, fasting, the eternal Word of God, and forming an unbreakable relationship with him will produce a love that will not be denied *total* allegiance to him. Christ, your Lord and King, deserves nothing less and will accept nothing less than complete allegiance. The Holy Spirit will cause you to become fully persuaded. Verse 32 says, "He who spared not His own son, but delivered him up for us all, how shall he not with him also freely give 'YOU' all things?" (emphasis supplied). It's time to be renewed in the spirit of your mind (Ephesians 4:23–24). It's time to resist all the gravitational pull of fear, doubt, unbelief, and even the insanity in believing that "it doesn't take of that." Multitudes are waiting to see this lifestyle operating in you. Be the leading force that will bring multitudes not only into the kingdom of God but also into this lifestyle of unshakable, undeniable allegiance to Christ. Welcome to the kingdom of God. **Read Acts 14:22.**

DAY 34

HIDE AND SEEK

But if from thence thou shalt seek the LORD thy God, thou shalt find him, if thou seek him with all thy heart and with all thy soul. (Deuteronomy 4:29)

The secret things belong to God, but those things revealed belong to us and our children. (Deut. 29:29)

Sometimes it seems as though God is hiding from us—no, that's a place where we learn to seek after him the more, hunger after Him the more. Desire His presence the more. Refuse to be denied. You need to come into such mature trust in God's promise that He will "never leave you or forsake you" (Hebrews 13:5a). "Seek first the kingdom of God and His righteousness and all these things shall be added unto you" (Matthew 6:33). The Greek word "seek" means to make something your primary pursuit or main concern, to search out specifically by worship or prayer. Persevering worship is in God's agenda for you. It's the passage to receive all things that belong to you in Christ Jesus. The place of this kind of "worship" is the place of obedience, like the obedience of Abraham when he was told to offer up his long-awaited promised one Isaac to God. Abraham told his servants, "Stay here at the foot of the mountain, I and the lad are going further up the mountain to 'worship.'" It wasn't to go and dance and shout around the altar as he was to tie his son down on the altar, kill him, and then set him on fire. That isn't a joyous occasion. Hebrews 11:17–18 declares Abraham's faith was so secure in the promise that it is stated in a figurative sense that he saw God raising him from the dead.

So allow the Holy Spirit to take you into a deeper soul search. See what place of your heart isn't yet given over to Him. Then release it in faith. He's waiting on your arrival.

DAY 35

VULNERABLE EMPOWERMENT

And I will very gladly spend and be spent for you; though the more abundantly I love you, the less I am loved. (2 Corinthians 12:15)

Only those who are hungry enough in their desire to walk in Christ's *greatness* can walk in this place without restraint. Love that is aggressive is given without restraint. Are you being prepared for this? Those who walk with Christ must learn to walk here! We have so received the love of God in Christ Jesus that there is no more fear in love. We have matured so in this unstoppable, unconditional love that the insanity of people and their present confusion cannot stop us from releasing the unshakable power of God's love. "Greater love has no man than this, than a man lay down his life for his friends. You are my friends if you do whatsoever I command you" (John 15:13–14). "By this shall all men know that you are my disciples, if you have love one to another" (John 13:35). Are you ready to walk in this force of love? The love of God that has been shed abroad in our hearts by the Holy Spirit has empowered us to withstand any attack of the enemy. Shut down the fear of being *hurt* by others. Stop trying to save your fleshly reputation, and allow only the reputation of Christ's name to be your place of honor. That's what we cover and protect. We are steadfast and committed to make sure *He* gets His dignity, honor, and respect back. Read 1 John 4:4–21.

DAY 36

THE TRUST FACTOR

You keep him in perfect peace whose mind is stayed on you, because he trusts in you. (Isaiah 26:3)

The depth of trust, brings the depth of peace, the depth of peace, brings the depth of soundness of mind, the depth of soundness of mind brings the depth of power!

This twenty-first *generation of Noah* is placing a demand on us as believers step up to the plate and honor the god we say we pray to. It's placing a demand in us to live by faith and stop responding to all this confusion by sight. We know how to rally together with picket signs and protest against quote "unrighteous" causes. But we can't rally together as a "body" of believers in prayer and shut down demonic forces in the heavenly realm. We must command the will of God to be done in the earth as it is already ordered in heaven. We must trust God to honor His Word because we know He cannot lie. God in Christ in us by the Holy Spirit is our peace. Not this world's system of peace. We must learn to master the Word of peace to live in the power of peace.

Where is your trust factor with God?

DAY 37

PURIYING THE SOUL

For the word of God is quick, and powerful, and sharper than any two edged sword, piercing even to the dividing asunder of soul and spirit, and of the joints and marrow, and is a discerner of the thoughts and intents of the heart. (Hebrews 4:12)

As we meditate on the Word of God and allow its penetrating power to continually divide asunder our soul and spirit, we will begin to recognize how our carnality was dominating in areas of our consciousness that's a hindrance to our spiritual growth and development. Now as we are being filled with the wisdom of God, the love of God, and the blessing of God, our words can pierce the atmosphere around us and bring the will of the kingdom of God into the earth as it is done in the heavens. This two-edged sword must first pierce our consciousness and asunder corrupt thinking into righteous thinking. We are made to bless others and not ridicule them, to build others up and not them down. In the body or outside of the body, we bless and do not curse. Life and death are in the power of our tongue. Our words pack power. Our words have creative power in them. So let us become so inundated with the living Word of God that the environment we live in will be greatly affected on a continual basis by creating God's will through His Word.

DAY 38

THE REALITY OF VICTORY

But thanks be to God, who gives us the victory through our Lord Jesus Christ. (1 Corinthians 15:57)

If our victory is sought out and gotten from any other source than Christ, then it's a lie and it will not stand. Every *today* is designed to challenge every *tomorrow*. Now yesterday's foolishness will challenge today's peace. Yesterday's prayerlessness will challenge today's place of power in prayer. Warriors of God, arise to your high calling in Christ Jesus. There's no place for carnality in the kingdom of God that's alive in us. We are a born-again spirit in Christ, and the Holy Spirit desires to perfect that which is in us by Father God. **Ephesians 2:10 says, "For we are his workmanship, created in Christ Jesus unto good works, which God has before ordained that we should walk in them."** Now that's powerful! It has already been established by the Father that we should live in this way. What are you waiting for? Possess your place in Him in the earth. It's your created position in Jesus Christ.

DAY 39

BEHOLDING THE GLORY

But we all, with open face beholding as in a glass the glory of the Lord, are changed into the same image from glory to glory, even as by the Spirit of the Lord. (2 Corinthians 3:18)

*D*o you believe you have already been glorified in Christ Jesus to give him glory in the earth by the life you live through Him each and every day of your existence in the earth? You must stop and meditate on these words from the apostle Paul in the book of Romans 8:30, "Moreover, whom he did predestinate, them He also called: and whom He called, them He also justified: and whom He justified them He also glorified."

These are not my words but the words of God's servant who wrote by experience and the inspiration of the Holy Spirit. Now it's up to you to examine God's Word of truth so that you can walk in the fullness of the measure of His son Christ Jesus. God cannot lie, so what He has spoken is already done. It's an eternal order that He desires for you to proudly and powerfully display in the earth. It's the order of His kingdom. See it, believe it, receive it; now be the expressed image of it before others. Read 2 Peter 1:2–11.

DAY 40

SUFFERING LAWFULLY

But if a man suffer as a Christian, let him not be ashamed; but let him glorify God in this name. (1 Peter 4:16)

We are the sold-out, sealed-to-serve, blood-washed sons of God. Bringing shame to our Lord's name is not an option! We are His glory to be revealed, His power to be demonstrated, and His goodness to be displayed at all times. **Second Timothy 3:12 declares, "Yes all who live godly in Christ Jesus shall suffer persecution."** This is an order between this side of eternity and the cross. It's a place in this life that we cannot escape. Let's back up to verses 10 and 11 and hear what Paul says concerning himself, **"But you have fully known my doctrine, manner of life, purpose, faith, longsuffering, love, patience, persecutions, afflictions, which came unto me at Antioch, at Iconium, at Lystra; what persecutions I endured: but out of them all the Lord delivered me."** Paul distinctly said out of them all, the Lord delivered him. The Word also declares that "God is no respecter of persons" (Acts 10:34). So if *all* are confronted with persecution, then *all* are delivered. **Isaiah 54:17** says that no weapon formed against us will prosper; every tongue that shall rise against us in judgment you shall condemn. Another translation says that we shall show to be in the wrong, which means we have been given the authority to condemn and declare unlawful any false accusations that are spoken against us. We can dispel it and shut it down. The weapon may be formed, but in the end, we will win; it cannot destroy us. We must learn to stand in the Word of God.

Read 2 Corinthians 4:7–11.

APOSTOLIC ORDER THROUGH THE WRITINGS OF PROVERBS

Here we have chosen key texts from the book of Proverbs that you can speak over your life daily. This is to establish divine wisdom into your consciousness by locking these truths into your subconscious mind. Faith is a spiritual order. Belief is of the mind. The more you establish the Word of God into your mind and spirit, *faith* comes alive. Faith *comes* by consistent hearing of the Word of God. Speak these words daily into your soul and spirit to become the living Word in divine wisdom and power.

Expectancy Commands Conformity, Conformity Brings Manifestation.
—Wisdom nuggets from Sias Wisdom Library

THE INTIMACY OF WISDOM

I am intimate with wisdom and instruction, and I grasp mentally and know thoroughly the words of wisdom. I receive instruction through wisdom, sound reasoning, decisive ability, and fairness. I teach others how to make sound decisions, have clear understanding, be well informed, and how to separate their unique difference from others. Because I am wise, I increase in learning and understand my need to always obtain wise counsel in major undertakings.

I recognize hidden truths, and wisdom aids in the correct interpretation of it. I honor those in authority and am able to receive instruction through the law of their mouth. I'm never enticed by the cunning words of the wicked no matter how lucrative their lives may seem, so I never partner with the unjust. I hear wisdom speaking in obscure places especially in the business of commerce to raise questions before the naive, the immature, those who scorn the good and hate knowledge.

I must understand if I ever refuse the voice of wisdom and laugh at wisdom's counsel, and despise the correction and instruction that wisdom brings, rest assured when I fall, wisdom will laugh at me. Wisdom will reject. So I seal in my memory this day, that whoever listens very carefully to wisdom will dwell in safety and be secure from evil.

ACCEPTING INSTRUCTION

To love instruction is to love knowledge. A good man obtains favor from the Lord. The root of the righteous is unmovable. A virtuous woman is a crown to her husband. My righteous thoughts are right, and my upright speech will always deliver me. In righteousness, my house will always stand. I will always be commended according to my wisdom. Wisdom calls for me to be diligent in all my endeavors. I must be diligent in business if I expect to profit. The just in God comes out of trouble because of sound words. I am satisfied with good by the fruit of my mouth, and the recompense of my hands shall be rendered unto me.

EQUALITY WISDOM FRUIT BEARING

Pride produces shame; there is always wisdom with the humble. Integrity is the guide of the upright, and perverseness destroys. Riches cannot profit in the time of danger, but righteousness delivers from death. The righteousness of the blameless shall direct his ways, and the upright shall be delivered. When it goes well with the righteous, the city rejoices, and when the wicked perish there is shouting. A man of understanding holds his peace; a talebearer tells all, but a man with a faithful spirit conceals the matter. The desire of the righteous is only good. We spread and increase our giving and it tends only to increase. The liberal soul shall be made fat, and he that waters is watered himself. A gracious woman retains honor and strong men retain riches. Blessings are upon the head of him that markets and sells his products to benefit the people. A fool is servant to the wise of heart. The righteous shall be recompensed in the earth.

THE TREASURES OF WISDOM

Receive the words of the wise as treasures in your heart, its commandments hidden within. You will listen carefully to wisdom and then apply your heart to understanding. Begin to cry out for knowledge and groan for understanding. Seek wisdom as for silver and search for understanding like hidden treasure; then godly fear shall be understood and the knowledge of God shall be found. Wisdom comes from God, from him also comes knowledge and understanding. A wise man stores up wisdom in undertaking good enterprise to substantiate the righteous in heart. God is also a shield to the upright. He guards the paths of justice in preserving the destiny of his saints. He gives us to understand righteousness, justice, equity, and every good path. Wisdom now enters our minds, and knowledge becomes pleasant to our soul. Discretion preserves my understanding and keeps me.

FOOLISHNESS VERSUS THE WISE IN HEART

A wife walks in wisdom to build her house and never tears it down. The wise walk in uprightness of heart because they fear God. We are always preserved because we speak only wise things. Much increase flows from the wise because God has made them with the strength of an ox. A faithful witness will not lie. The wise have understanding; therefore, knowledge comes easily to and through them. Do not stay in the atmosphere of foolish men for they lack knowledge. We are wise, we are prudent, and we understand our way in life. We live in and among the righteous where favor abides. We do not live in the rage of self-confidence because we fear God and always depart from evil. The gate of the righteous stands strong, for it is the place where evil and wickedness bow.

JOY IN WISDOM

    I must always respond with a soft answer to turn away wrath and grievous words. My wise tongue will always use knowledge in the right way. The eyes of the Lord are in every place, seeing good and evil. The wholesomeness of my speech will be a tree of life, and a perverse tongue will always cause separation. If I receive and apply strong correction, I remain prudent and sensible. The house of the righteous is full of treasure, and their speech always spreads knowledge. Keep me upright, Lord, so that my prayers will always be your delight. I follow hard after righteousness and my father loves me. My heart is always before the Lord; nothing is hidden from him. Slothfulness brings thorns, but righteousness keeps my path plain.

COUNSELORS INCREASE LEARNING

A man of understanding walks uprightly. I desire to keep many counselors around me so that my purposes are established and not disappointed. I bring joy by the answers of my mouth, and wise counsel in the right season is wonderful. I seek the wisdom that is from heaven that keeps me from destruction. The words of the pure in heart are always pleasant to the Lord. Hate bribes and lives; seeking fast money brings trouble. My heart is quick to study and answer and not just blurt out anything. My ear hears the reproofs of life and keeps me living among the wise. If I refuse instruction, I despise my own; if I take heed to reproof, I receive understanding. To fear the Lord is instruction operating out of wisdom, and before I can walk in honor I must first learn to be humble.

POWER IN SONSHIP

As a wise son, I give full attention to obedience and discernment. I make proclamations by listening attentively to my heavenly Father's instructions. I will always eat, partake of, and enjoy good by the fruit of my mouth. Learning to guard my words, I will always preserve my life. If I am slothful in business, I will have nothing. It is my diligence that makes me fat. The righteous hate lying. I must guard against selfishness in riches and always reach toward others. The covering seal on my life are riches obtained by the instruction of fathers. If I stay well advised, I stay wise. By fearing the father's commandment, I am rewarded. The law of wisdom is my fountain of life, keeping me from the snares of death. Having a good understanding keeps me gaining in favor for my life.

MEN PLAN BUT GOD DIRECTS

The plans of the heart belong to man, but the instructions of the mouth belong to God. He must speak to direct your paths. A man's ways are pure in himself, but God judges the spirit. Commit your plans to God, roll it over on him, and he will establish your thoughts. The Lord made everything for himself; even wickedness is to his advantage. Pride is disgusting to God; you may join up with others, but you will not escape punishment. My heart may plan one thing, but God directs my steps. A divine sentence is in my mouth, and I will not transgress in judgment. God's concern is that all negotiations are handled with equality and character. The place of authority is established by righteousness and not wickedness. The weighing of choices is set by men, but the final decision belongs to the Lord. Wisdom teaches me what to say and adds learning to how I say it.

CONTENTMENT YIELDS PEACE

I'm better off with a little bit in an atmosphere of peace than to have abundance in an atmosphere of strife. Even a servant, if he is wise, will rule over the son's inheritance. There are natural things that purify silver and gold, but it is God that purifies the heart of man. The wicked obeys false lips, and liars listen to destructive words. Never mock the poor; it is a reproach to God. It's destructive to laugh at calamities. Children and grandchildren are a crown to the aged, and the glory of children are the fathers. Fools don't speak with excellence, and lies should not be in the mouth of a prince. Rewards are very precious; it brings redemptive value to prosper at every direction. Love covers transgressions; speaking them can destroy the best of friendships. I would rather meet a bear whose cubs were stolen than to meet a fool bound in foolishness.

WISDOM GIVES ATTENTION TO DETAILS

Never reward evil for good, for evil shall not depart from your house. Don't start an argument; it's like opening a faucet of confusion, so just cut it off before it starts. A foolish person will never pay the price to get wisdom; it's not their mind-set. It seems as though a friend can love you always, and those in your own bloodline are always against you. Cosigners and people who become guarantors for others are empty in their understanding. Joy in the heart is like medicine, and a broken spirit will dry you up. Taking bribes to correct a right is utter wickedness. I have knowledge; therefore, my words are few and I have understanding and I keep an excellent spirit. Even fools that hold back, their tongues are considered wise, and he that shuts his lips is esteemed as a person of understanding. What about you?

WISDOM: THE PRINCIPAL THING

Listen to the instructions of a father and attend to know understanding. Let your heart retain his words of wisdom. Keep his commandments and live. Get wisdom, get understanding to not forget it. Never decline from the words of his mouth. Never forsake wisdom, and wisdom shall keep you. Wisdom is the most important thing; therefore, get wisdom and in all, you're getting get an understanding. Exalt wisdom and wisdom will promote you. Wisdom will bring you to honor when you learn to embrace it. Wisdom will become like an ornament of grace on your head. A crown of glory will be given to you. Receive your father's sayings and the years of your life shall be many. Always receive instruction. Hold it close to you and never let it go for it is your life. Guard and protect your soul with perseverance, with painstaking effort. For out of your soul come the boundaries of life.

THE VOICE OF WISDOM

The cry of wisdom with understanding brings forth a voice. Wisdom is heard in the high places of commerce and weighty transactions. Wisdom speaks to the seats of authority in cities and high places of rule when chief decisions must be made. Wisdom cries out to the sons of man. Wisdom speaks to the simple in heart, pleading with the foolish to become of an understanding heart. Wisdom desires to speak excellent things. Wisdom speaks of truth and righteousness, never wickedness nor perverseness. Receive instruction over silver and knowledge rather than precious gold. Wisdom is better than the finest of jewelry. There is nothing that can be desired that can be compared to wisdom. Wisdom dwells with prudence and finds out knowledge of witty inventions. Counsel is mine and sound wisdom. Wisdom has understanding. Wisdom has strength.

THE ORDER OF QUEENS

The words of a queen are prophetic in nature to build, instruct, council, and correct. The words of a queen can keep the hearts of kings in their rightful order. King Lemuel was inspired to write the instructions of his mother's words that directed his placement as a king in the earth and to establish his kingdom in power. My son! Son of my womb! Son of my vows! It is not the order of kings to give their power and influence to women. Do not give your honor to that which will destroy you. It is not the place for you to drink alcohol; getting drunk on wine causes you to become confused in judging with righteousness. You forget true law and order and become lawless in standing for those who are afflicted. Strong drink is for those who are perishing. They drink to forget their life of misery.

Open your mouth for those who cannot speak for themselves to keep them from destruction. Open your mouth and stand in the place of righteousness in behalf of the poor and needy. It's the woman of virtue that's fit for a king. The investments to be made in her are far above rubies. You must be willing to safely trust in her so that there is no spoil in your life, knowing she will do you good and not evil all the days of your life. She's full of witty inventions; she's an entrepreneur at heart not afraid to work hard to bring her dreams to pass. She's willing to do what others will not do to be a blessing on earth. She supplies for the poor and needy also, and she's not afraid of difficulty or hardship. She's a person of excellence and demands the best in all she sets her hand to do. Her husband is known in the key places of authority and power.

Wisdom is a strong virtue in her life, and kindness is a law of life expressed continually. You and the children she has given you always call her blessed. Together you praise her and show her your deep appreciation for her life. She is a woman who fears the Lord; she must be praised. Her own works will be known in key places of power in the earth.

WHY APOSTOLIC PRAYERS?

Why apostolic prayers, you might ask? If we are going to witness "true revival" on earth, we must return to the root cause. What was happening in the Body of Christ during the times of true revival that was clearly defined and witnessed, clearly seen and demonstrated. We have to start with the early ecclesia. This civil judicial governing body of believers gave their lives for the preaching of the Gospel. The word *warfare* in 1 Corinthians 10:4 is interpreted as "engaging the apostolic," contending with carnal inclinations to serve in a military campaign, the apostolic career one of hardship and danger.

This doesn't, by any means, describe the Church of Jesus Christ today! We have been duped into a "Laodicea" state. We have become drunk with the wine of Babylon, and it's time for radical change. It's time to get on our face and cry out to God for a real revival to take place in us as individuals so that a collective "body language" can be heard. The prophet Isaiah spoke in chapter 9:6 that "the government [empire] shall be upon His [Christ] shoulder." We are the "shoulder," not shoulders (plural), but *shoulder*— singular. We are one powerful, global entity to be reckoned with.

So we must return to living by the Apostles' Doctrine, the doctrine of the chief apostle and high priest Christ Jesus. This is the pattern Lucifer has tried to shut down and destroy. How can you destroy an eternal order?

The *world* of the believer has no end. Return to your *first creative order*, the true new creation in Christ Jesus who is Lord of all.

The Governor Apostle,

Apostle D.W. Sias

KEY APOSTOLIC PRAYERS AND PROPHETIC PROMISES

Pray for revelation of Jesus's beauty that we might walk in our calling and destiny by God's power. "That … the Father of glory, may give to you the spirit of wisdom and revelation in the knowledge of Him, the eyes of your understanding being enlightened; that you may *know* [experience] what is the hope of His calling [assurance or clarity of God's call for our life], what are the riches of the glory of His inheritance in the saints [our destiny as Jesus's inheritance], and what is the exceeding greatness of His power toward us who believe, according to the working of His mighty power" (Ephesians 1:17–19).

Pray to receive the Spirit's power so that Jesus's presence would be manifested in us, so we experience God's love. "*That* [emphasis added] He would grant you, according to the riches of His glory, to be strengthened with might through His Spirit in the inner man; *that* [emphasis added] Christ may dwell [manifest His presence] in your hearts through faith; *that* [emphasis added] you, being rooted and grounded in love, may be able to comprehend [experience] with all the saints what is the breadth, and length, and depth, and height; to know the love of Christ, which passes knowledge *that* [emphasis added] you may be filled with all the fullness of God" (Ephesians 3:16–19).

Pray for God's love to abound in us by the knowledge of God, resulting in righteousness in our lives. "That your love may abound still more and more in knowledge [of God] and all judgment that you may approve [rejoice in] the things that are excellent; that you may be sincere [no compromise] and without offence till the day of Christ. Being filled with the fruits of righteousness" (Philippians 1:9–11).

Pray to know God's will to be fruitful in ministry and strengthened by intimacy with Him. "That you may be filled with the knowledge of His will in all wisdom and spiritual understanding; that you may have a walk worthy of the Lord, fully pleasing, being fruitful in every good work and increasing in the knowledge of God; strengthened with all might, according to His glorious power, for all patience and longsuffering with joy" (Colossians 1:9–11).

Pray for unity in the Church and to be filled with supernatural joy, peace, and hope (confidence). "Now the God of patience and comfort grant you to be likeminded toward one another … that you may, with one mind and one mouth glorify the … Father … Now the God of hope fill you with all joy and peace in believing, that you may abound in hope, through the power of the Holy Ghost" (Romans 15:5–6, 13).

Pray to be enriched by all the gifts of the Spirit, including powerful preaching and prophetic revelation. "That you are enriched in everything by Him, in all utterance [anointed preaching or singing] and all knowledge [prophetic revelation], even as the testimony of Christ was confirmed in you [by miracles], so that you come behind in no gift, waiting for the coming of

… Jesus Christ, who shall also confirm you unto the end, that you may be blameless in the day of our Lord Jesus Christ" (1 Corinthians 1:5–8).

Pray for the release of grace to bring the Church to maturity and especially to abound in love and holiness. "Praying exceedingly that … [God will release His Spirit and grace to] perfect that which is lacking in your faith … And [may] the Lord make you to increase and abound in love [to one another and to all] … that He may establish your hearts unblameable in holiness before [our] God [and] … Father" (1 Thessalonians 3:10–13).

Pray to be worthy (prepared or made spiritually mature) to walk in the fullness of our destiny in God. "We pray always for you, that our God would count you worthy of [and prepare us for] this calling, and fulfil all the good pleasure of His goodness [plans for us] and the work of faith with power: That the name of … Jesus may be glorified in you, and you in Him, according to the grace of our God" (2 Thessalonians 1:11–12).

That the Word will increase its influence (effectiveness) in the city as God releases His power on it. "Pray for us, that the word of the Lord may have free course, [rapidly increase its influence] and be glorified [confirmed with apostolic power and miracles], even as it is with you ... The Lord is faithful, who shall establish you, and keep you from evil ... [May] the Lord direct your hearts into the love of God and into the patient waiting [perseverance or endurance] for Christ" (2 Thessalonians 3:1–5).

For impartation of boldness (singing and speaking the Word) by releasing healing, signs, and wonders. "Lord ... grant unto your servants ... [that] with all boldness [they may speak your word by stretching out] ... your hand to heal; and that signs and wonders may be done through the name of your holy Servant Jesus. And when they had prayed, the place was shaken where they were assembled together; and they were all filled with the Holy Spirit, and they spoke the word of God with boldness" (Acts 4:29–31).

A. Release of God's promise to be endued with power for all who tarry (labor in prayer) for breakthrough. "Behold, I send the promise of My Father upon you; but tarry in the city of Jerusalem until you are ... [endued] with power from on high ... He lifted up His hands and blessed them" (Luke 24:49–50).

For the Lord to release His zeal for His people and for His manifest presence to shake all that resists Him. "Look down ... and see from your habitation, holy and glorious. Where are [the manifestations of] your zeal and your strength, the yearning of your heart and your mercies toward me? ... You, O Lord, are our Father, our redeemer; from Everlasting is your name ... Oh, that you would rend the heavens! That you would come down [manifest your power]! That the mountains (obstacles) might shake at Your presence— as fire burns brushwood, as fire causes water to boil—to make Your name known to Your adversaries [sin, sickness, Satan], that the nations may tremble at Your presence! When you did awesome things for which we did not look (expect) ... Since the beginning of the world men have not heard ... nor has the eye seen any God besides You, who acts for the one who waits for Him. You meet him who rejoices and does righteousness, who remembers you in your ways" (Isaiah 63:15–16; 64:1–7).

For the release of God's promise to pour out His Spirit and release dreams, visions, and prophecy. "In the last days, says God, that I will pour out of My Spirit on all flesh: your sons and your daughters shall prophesy, your young men shall see visions, your old men shall dream dreams ... On My servants and on my handmaidens I will pour out My Spirit [in those days]; and they shall prophesy ... I will show wonders in heaven above, and signs in the earth beneath: blood, and fire, and vapour of smoke: The sun shall be turned into darkness, and the moon into blood, *before* [emphasis added] the coming of the great and awesome day of the Lord. Whoever calls on the name of the *Lord* [emphasis added] shall be saved" (Acts 2:17–21).

Prayer for Israel to be saved and the release of the prophetic anointing, miracles, and righteousness. "My heart's desire and prayer to God for Israel is, that they may be saved" (Romans 10:1).

"All Israel will be saved ... The Deliverer [Jesus] will come out of Zion. He will turn away ungodliness from Jacob: For this is My covenant with them, when I take away their sins" (Romans 11:26–27).

"For Zion's sake I will not hold my peace [be silent; release a prophetic spirit], and for Jerusalem's sake I will not rest [or I will not be inactive: release power], *until* her righteousness [in all heart issues] goes forth as brightness, and her salvation as a lamp that burns [ministry to others]" (Isaiah 62:1).

Prayers taken from Mike Bickle Ministries (apostolic prayers).